The Democrats: The Party for Minorities and Masters of Illusions.

INTRODUCTION

I once saw a cartoon drawing that attempted to show the difference between Democrats and Republicans. The drawing was actually two panels side by side. On one side was the Democrats and the other side was the Republicans. In each panel there was a drawing of a pit (hole in the ground) with a crowd of people inside the pit. On the democrats side, a group of Democrats outside and above the pit was yelling at each other to *"Bring more food!"* while on the Republican side, the group of Republicans outside and above the pit was yelling at each other to *"Bring more ladders!"*

To me, each side has their positive and negative connotations: *"You need help (ladders) to move upwards and you need nourishment (food) to climb the ladder."*

Neither party is 100% right or 100% wrong. Let me make this perfectly clear. The Republicans are not

1

100% right but neither are they 100% wrong. The Democrats are not 100% right but neither are they 100% wrong.

If you believe that your party is 100% gospel. Then maybe this book is not for you.

This book is addressed to the thinking man and women of minorities.

I have decided to write this book on the Democrats because it is the majority party affiliated with minorities. Among the majority of minorities, the word "Democratic" is a word that is associated in good terms whereas the word "Republican" is not.

The Definition of an illusion is: 1. something that deceives by producing a false or misleading impression of reality. **2.** The state or condition of being deceived; misapprehension. In Psychology, it is defined as "a perception that represents what is perceived in a way different from the way it is in reality."

I will make the argument that minorities in the inner cities have been deluded to believe that the Democratic ideology is best for them. In some areas of the nation, the inners cities filled with minorities have been under Democrats control for 60 and in some cases for 110 years. Newark New Jersey has had Democrat Mayor since 1907!

The Democrats have been so successful in implementing this illusion of well being in the minds of minorities that we, in leaving a Democrat area for a better life elsewhere, will actually vote Democrat again inviting the same ideology that ruined the neighborhood that we ran away from in the first place. We are totally brainwashed. Even the top liberal Democrat leaders live in Republican Conservative areas **or** in the best neighborhoods of the area they represent fully protected from the inner cities lifestyles that they control. The inner cities are the end results of Democrats ideologies and they continue to manipulate minorities into whatever use they need from us. Whether it is to make us placid with handouts, allow proliferation of crime and drugs, make us spendthrift (consumerism) or incite us to violence when they are voted out of office, they continue with the help of their allies in the media and Hollywood to use us as their puppets. I will contest in this book that we (minorities) have accepted this political party without reasoning. It is my aim to urge minorities to use their power of reasoning. Too long has the votes of minorities been taken for granted because the default mindset is to vote Democrat. As minorities we cannot allow our votes to be taken for granted nor should we be satisfied with the "scrapes from the master's table" in exchange for our votes.

Knowledge is power only when you apply it in your life. You stand with Knowledge and you walk with wisdom.

The Democrats: The Party for Minorities and Masters of Illusions.

THE ILLUSION

I am going to describe two incidents that happened to me that are examples of the illusions that the Democrats have successfully perpetuated upon minorities:

First Example: I was walking with a couple of friends in a middle class neighborhood in Brooklyn one summer afternoon. Both are stanch liberal democrats. I commented how nice this neighborhood is and that one day I hope to have a beautiful home like these. They immediately broke out in laughter by remarking that I am Hispanic and joked that I was trying to be white.

Question: Is the person who calls you a racist, the racist because he was the first to see things in terms of color or race? Is the accuser the color minded person?

Second Example: I attended a teacher-student conference with my girl friend for her son at the catholic school he was attending in Brooklyn. As I sat quietly in one of their classroom, I became aware that the classroom itself brought me memories of my own childhood school classrooms: *The wooden desk with the pencil groove on top, words of wisdom posted on the walls by American leaders, the Ten Commandments, sayings of Proverbs, world maps, etc.*

These things were in my public schools during the time of my schooling. Schooling was about education and developing the child's character and morals. Nowadays, the public school system in minority neighborhoods are a mess and crime is rampant with many parents fearing for their child. Teachers are social experimenting with an education that is liberal leaning. So a parent who disagrees with this liberal ideology must find another educational institution like a Catholic School to educate her child. My girl friend was paying over $6000.00 per year (at the time) to get a quality education and without fear of violence. At one time, when schools in the inner cities were mostly of a European/Caucasian majority,

the free public schools system was like the present day Catholic School system. Now minorities have to pay tuition (besides paying the millage tax for the local school board) at a private school for a quality character building education if they want to avoid attending the failed local public schools that they are locked into.

Question: Why does the Pro-Democrat leaning Teacher's Union supports the prevention of minority parents choosing to leave a failed school and allow them better school choice for their child? Why do they want us to be locked into a failed school system? Why are they opposed to School Choice?

Why does the Pro-Democrat Teacher's Union force feed the children of poor minority parents Transgender ideology, Two Mommies or Two Daddies households, Homosexuality and other teachings that conflict with the religious beliefs of the parents? It's not that the parents have a choice for their child whether to take the class or not; its' forced on them. This can cause conflict between the parent and the child along with the undue financial burden if the parent decides to enroll in a private school because of this conflict. Only the more affluential will have that option. If the parent, who just wants their child to have a good education consisting of Reading, Writing and Arithmetic, tries to resist these ideologies, they are labeled by the Democrats "racist" "ignorant" "uninformed" "homophobic" and other unfair labels resulting in minority neighborhoods segmented against each other. One side labeled as "hate group" and the other side as the "enlightened group." Some minority parents just want to be left alone and not have their child be subject to this kind of social experimental engineering by liberal educators.

There are many ways of destroying a people or a movement. There is nothing new under the sun. From Scriptures to Saul Alinsky to the psychology of deceptive maneuvers, there are many ways to destroy a people or a movement to such a subliminal extent that the people or movement will actually welcome and support it! Let me detail one way I call **"Self- Imposed Segmental Racism"** that has been employed by the Democratic Party upon minorities without us being conscience of it. Here is an example of **"Self- Imposed Segmental Racism:"**

"Let's say I want to achieve stronger controls over a certain group of people. Let's say for argument sake that I want to increase my domination, for whatever twisted reasoning that I have, over the Irish people

yet attain their votes so I can remain in power. I will first, with the help of my party and my allies, jump in front in support of all issues relating to Irish concerns. I will champion their causes, speak in favor, and embrace all things "IRISH" while anyone that doesn't, I will label them a racist and not a friend of the Irish people. I will be front and center on all Irish issues that are pressing to the quality of life to the Irish people like education, security, crime, jobs, business entrepreneurship, etc. But I would also mix in issues that I know will lower the quality of life among them like the rights of the criminals, lowering the standards of education for the naive, fostering federal dependency for single parenthood, calling for the victimization of the slothful and entitlement from the productive, increase regulations and taxation on Irish businesses, support for the most undesirable traits in the Irish community by labeling them victims of an unfair society, etc.

As I move forward, I will continuously silence any opposition by calling on Unity, Love and Support for the Irish. All others who object to my intentions would be branded a traitor, a racist, an uncle tom, xenophobe, etc.

Meanwhile and without my objections, my allies in Hollywood would glamorize the more deviant life styles (like Hollywood has done in the past) within the Irish culture. My friends in the Music industry will do the same and my liberal Media supporters would either ignore these problems or spin stories of support for these deviant life styles by stimulating emotionalism for them. Hollywood, Music Industry and the Media will of course be far removed from the real life that is affecting the Irish. Together, these allies of mine would continue to foster an image in the minds of the Irish young that sensationalizes the negative element among them. Eventually, the good among the Irish will demand more regulations and better protection in attempt to stop or protect themselves from these negative influences in their society. Of course I and my allies will be there with solutions coupled with more restrictions to further create segmentation, control and regulation all in the name of liberty and progress."

Some can say that this is "divide and conquer" but this is more devious. This is dividing and conquering with the people <u>willingly</u> welcoming the solution to their issues from the same people who created the problem to begin with. The Democrats create the problem then we come to them for help with issues that they implanted from the start. This is the fox guarding the hen house. This is the wolf in sheep's clothing.

We make a mistake to accept the premise that the Democrat Party is what you see and hear from the leaders of the Democrat party. The Democrat Party is just a front. The real Democrat party is the financial and power supporters. The real Democrat Party is Hollywood, Music Industry, Silicon Valley, the Educational System, Teacher's Union, Labor Unions, Wall Street, Pharmaceuticals industry, Liberal News Media, Soros minions, Talk shows and late shows and the powerful elites in the Justice System and government agencies. What makes them unified against Republicans and Conservatives is their belief that they are fighting on the side of righteousness. To them it's good vs. evil; they are the good and Republicans are evil. How did this happen? It happened because they were successful through the use of their allies to freeze, paint, and define Republicans as racist, greedy, insensitive, uncaring, xenophobic, sexist, fascist, un-evolved and ignorant. Minorities have come to depend on the Democrats for salvation and progress while not recognizing the coordinated destruction of minorities by the Democrat allies.

Question: Why did the Pharmaceutical Companies support Obama-care?

In a May 25, 2013 article written in forbes.com by Bruce Japsen, below is a clip of his article:

"Obamacare Will Bring Drug Industry $35 Billion in Profits. Despite expiring patents on blockbuster drugs and a wave of new regulation from the Affordable Care Act that will cost drug makers, the pharmaceutical industry will reap between "$10 billion and $35 billion in additional profits over the next decade," a new analysis shows. The health law, which will bring millions of uninsured Americans health benefits beginning in January 2014, will be a critical boon to pharmaceutical industry balance sheets, increasing revenue by one-third by the end of the decade, according to a new report from research and consulting firm GlobalData of London. That means the U.S. pharmaceutical industry's market value will mushroom by 33 percent to $476 billion in 2020 from $359 billion last year."

Follow the money. It's all about the money. The Democrats will always come across as if they care for your welfare but the truth is they care about Power and they care about the Money that will support their Power.

- **<u>President John Kennedy speech</u>**

Go to YouTube and hear President John Kennedy speech "The President and the Press" given before the American Newspaper Publishers Association on April 27, 1961.

Question: Why should this speech be a concern to minorities and what does it have to do with the illusion that Democrats love to perpetrate on minorities? The answer will come to you. Continue reading.

In his speech, President Kennedy warns the American People by saying, *"we are opposed around the world by a monolithic and ruthless conspiracy that relies primarily on covert means for expanding its sphere of influence. On infiltration instead of invasion; on subversion instead of elections; on intimidation instead of free choice; on guerillas by night instead of armies by day. It is a system which has conscripted vast human and material resources into the building of a tightly knit highly efficient machine that combines military, diplomatic, intelligence, economic scientific and political operations. Its preparations are concealed, not published. Its mistakes are buried not headlined. Its dissenters are silenced, not praised. No expenditure is question, no rumor is printed, no secret is revealed."*

Who is President Kennedy speaking about? Who would have such power? Think about the fact that the majority of American Newspaper is democrat left liberal leaning. Think about the fact that today's main stream media is 99.9% democrat left liberal leaning. Think about the fact that Hollywood, the Music Industry, College Professors, Teachers Union, Labor Unions, Wall Street Titans, Soros Minions, Silicon Valley and Pharmaceuticals are all democrat left liberal leaning. Their greater part of their fiscal donation is to the Democrat Party.

President Kennedy is talking about a one world government, a world without borders: A world with one supreme government, one army, one political party, one police force, one country, one currency, one world power. This is called "Globalism." Another name that is used for this belief is "Corporate Globalism" because mega corporations will be the economic engine driving this concept while the controlling political party would be the driver in charge. The liberal Democrats are perfectly willing (and encouraged) to be the driver in charge. To achieve this goal, they need the support of the heavy hitters of our society. The heavy hitters are the Corporate Giants, Wall Street, Pharmaceuticals, Teachers Union, Labor Unions, Silicon Valley, Main Stream Media, Hollywood, Talk Show Hosts, Soros minions, College Professors, and the Justice System to name a few. All of these entities are strong supporters of the Democrat Party. These heavy hitters support by way of money and through activism the ideology of Liberalism and Corporate Globalism. Some support it willingly; some unwillingly to avoid the pressure from the powerful entities that are in the Globalist Camp. To accomplish the Globalist goals, they need to eliminate borders and abolish the unique characteristics of a country and its culture.

Below are **8 examples** that can easily be found on the internet that reveals a surreptitious attempt to create a one world globalist utopia:

1). In a 2003 speech delivered to Yale University, Bill Clinton called for the establishment of a "global community," praised the "openness of our borders to immigrants," and declared that America "has great obligations to open our borders." Clinton said that he believes the formation of a "genuine global community"—complete with an "over-arching system" to regulate it—to be "the great mission of the 21st century."

2). In July 2007, Bill Clinton praised the benefits of "open borders" and "easy immigration" while delivering the keynote address at the 16th Telugu Association of North America

3). In closed-door remarks delivered to a foreign bank, Hillary Clinton declared that her "dream is a hemispheric common market, with open trade and open borders: "My dream is a hemispheric common market, with open trade and open borders.." [05162013 Remarks to Banco Itau.doc, p. 28]

4). Speaking at Northeastern University commencement ceremonies on May 13, 2016, Secretary of State John Kerry called for a "borderless world."

5). Obama's "catch and release" program of illegal and sometimes dangerous immigrants being released back on American soil under the guise of freedom was nothing more than to supplement Democrats' voter rolls and place undue financial hardships on states. This would entice the states to request and become recipients for federal funding. This funding with strings attached will make the state subservient to federal rules and regulations which would further cement a centralized federal power over the states.

6). Obama sought that global entities have greater control of the internet. Following is a clipping of an email by a reader on this subject: *"On October 1st a critical portion of the management of the Internet, the IANA, which handles, among other things, the allocation of IP addresses (the gateway to the Internet), will fall under international control {NTIA, 2016}. Because of the involved exemption of antitrust laws, which allows for a monopoly of the involved technology and services, this critical infrastructure is required to have some form of governmental oversight to operate {Wall Street Journal, 2016}. Thus far that oversight has been conducted by the United States Government, but by ceding control of this critical component of the Internet to international control, US citizens will necessarily be monitored by an international body (likely the UN over the course of time) {Wall Street Journal, 2016}. As this strategic entity acts as the gatekeeper to the Internet, it is reasonable to assume that censorship, according to international norms, can be expected on a global scale to include the citizens of the USA."* The censorship, of course, will be anyone that does not believe in the Democrat ideology.

7). Leaked documents from George Soros' Open Society Foundation show that the organization's goal behind funding the Black Lives Matter movement is ultimately to federalize America's police forces. The document is aptly called, "Police Reform: How to Take Advantage of the Crisis of the Moment and Drive Long-Term Institutional Change in Police-Community Practice." Soros is a billionaire financier who gives billions to left-wing causes and wants to curtail American sovereignty. Soros would like nothing better than for America to become subservient to international bodies. Soros is a pro-liberal Democrat.

8). China is calling for a global currency to replace the dominant dollar, showing a growing assertiveness on revamping the world economy. They are buying up Hollywood and other Technological Companies.

Remember the Star Trek movie about the Borgs? For those that are not familiar with the Borg, they are part organic and part artificial beings. They assimilate almost everyone they come in contact with. They would absorb their victims into the Borg which is a consciousness that made victims into drones who would not remember their old life. Your individual life as you knew it was no longer true once assimilated. The favorite Borg quote is: "*We are the Borg. Lower your shields and surrender your ships. We will add your biological and technological distinctiveness to our own. Your culture will adapt to service us. Resistance is futile.*" Once assimilated, you become a small part of the collective and lose all sense of individuality. This is the way of the Democrats. You either assimilate or get destroyed.

Democrats say they love the working class people. Democrats love us so much that they love putting us all into little categories so to better address our issues. It is here that we give them power over us. Tyrants always come in the name of the working class people. Minorities in the Democrat Party better toe the line because if you don't, you are labeled a "coconut" (black outside, white inside), an Uncle Tom, a sell-out, ignorant, etc. These labels are enforced by their allies in the media and Hollywood. Democrats do not see humans and its economy as a viable dynamic living entity growing and cultivating with the creativity of our God given potential. They see the economy as a finite pie: the bigger your slice, the smaller for everyone else. Of course this doesn't apply to them because they keep growing in wealth and power. Democrats see the worlds' occupants as something to control and maneuver for the collective good. The Collective mindset is the Corporate Globalist ideology. The Democrats and their allies see themselves evolved enough to make the laws and be in charge for the greater collective.

WHY SHOULD THIS CONCERN MINORITIES?

Did you see the Hungry Games Trilogy? You remember how the world was made up? The powers in charge broke the country up in segments. Each segment knew its place and position. Each segment worked for the government. Out of our two party systems (Republicans and Democrats) which party can you identify this hungry games scenario? The answer can only be the Democrats. Why? Because they are the ones who love placing sections of society in segments and then teach us to hate the opposing segments: *Rich vs Poor; Educated vs Uneducated; Black vs White; Immigrants vs Citizens; Police vs Criminals; Atheism vs Religion; Gays vs Straight; Anarchy vs Civility; Democrats vs Republicans; Labor vs Business; Individual Rights vs Majority Rights.* Then the Democrats teach us that it is only <u>they</u> that can protect us against your opposing segment.

Imagine if the Democrats ideology of Globalism succeeds. I ask my minority brothers and sisters, what will happen to you? How will you fit into this world of theirs? Would the Corporate Globalist relegate minorities to a culture of consumerism (spendthrifts) like the Democrats and their allies have been doing to minorities since emancipation. Go online and research the many articles on Black Consumerism. Read its history and the impact on

African American communities and other minority groups. Isn't it Hollywood, the Entertainment Industry and the Music Industry that stimulates and fosters consumerism? Which political party do they support and contribute to? The answer is the Democrats. Read "The explosion of consumerism in Western Europe" ... - Tufts University. *ase.tufts.edu/gdae/CS/Explosion.pdf*

On September 14, 2000, Dr. Claude Anderson, President of Harvest Institute speaking on "Reparations for Slavery" on C-Span2 said, *"During slavery, our ancestors owned 1.5% of American wealth. Today, over 150 years later and all the freedom we can imagine, we still only own 1.5% of American wealth in this country. Does that sound like we are making any progress?"*

It's interesting that the Democrat Mayors have had control of our inner cities for 60 to 100 plus years in some instances. According to Wikipedia under the title of "Political power in the United States over time" it quotes that 'over the past 100 years the Democratic party has held power nearly twice as long as the Republicans in both the Senate and the House. And the Democratic Party has had control of the White House and the two Houses of Congress for 35 years, compared to 16 years for the Republican

Party over the last 100 years.' **Wikipedia further breaks down the statistics over the past 100 years from 1916 to 2015:**

Senate control: Democrats 56 years; Republicans 34 years.

Congress control: Democrats 65 years; Republicans 35 years.

Control of both the Senate and Congress: Democrats 57 years; Republicans 27 years.

Control of the Senate, Congress and the Presidency: Democrats 35 years; Republicans 16 years.

Control of the Presidency: Democrats 52 years; Republicans 48 years.

The facts speak for themselves. The Democrats and the illusions that have been perpetrated upon the minds of minorities have kept minorities from economic freedom and financial wealth. They are the party that claims they are for the poor so it stands to reason that they need to keep you poor in order to stay in power.

Would the schools under the Pro-Democrat Teachers Union teach minorities' economic development and self-reliance or will they teach us "non-economic liberalism" pushing us towards acceptance of Hollywood's cultural image of minorities for social integration as the school system does now on minorities. Study the history of the NAACP & Non-Economic Liberalism.

Maybe the Liberal Democrats will finally have the power to silence and destroy companies that try to maintain their religious obligations in their business practices like NYC Mayor Bill de Blasio tried to do when he called for a boycott of Chic-fil-a because he called biblical massages that Chic-fil-a was placing on their packages about their views on marriages as "Hate Speech."

Or worse, maybe if the liberal Democrats had total control of the political spectrum, perhaps they will force women to give up their newborns to strange couples in hopes of ending racism. This idea was actually presented in 2017 by Howard Rachlin, research professor of Psychology at Stony Brook University and Marvin Frankel, professor of Psychology at Sarah Lawrence College in an article entitled, "If Babies were randomly allocated to families would racism end?" Just imagine if they had the power of the Global Government behind them to enforce this idea. It's not that far fetch when you consider that minorities were used for medical experimentation driven entirely by the Secretary of Public Health of the US federal Government under the administration of Democrat President Harry S. Truman on the African American population in Tuskegee Alabama from 1932 through 1972. The lists of Alabama Governors and Mayors from 1932 through 1972 were all Democrats. This list includes the infamous Gov. George Wallace. This experimentation was called the Tuskegee syphilis experiment during which approximately 400 African American Men (who affected their wives) was under the illusion that they were being treated for syphilis but the reality was that they were used as guinea pigs for study on how untreated syphilis affects the body. They were not informed of this nor treated even though the standard treatment for syphilis was penicillin by 1947. The physician who was involved with this study was Democrat physician John Charles Cutler. In another experiment on the Latin people of Guatemala, Mr. Cutler infected approximately 1500 men, women and children with the syphilis bacterium.

What remedy will we have as minorities if Democrat's global corporate ideology is realized supported and promulgated by their allies in Hollywood and the media. Who would be able to stand against such power? Remember President

Kennedy's speech! The one world government and its tentacles would be too powerful to fight.

Remember: **Power corrupts. Total power corrupts totally.**

Or maybe they can continue the massacre of minority babies under the guise of women's liberty and family planning supported by liberal educators and Hollywood.

Below is a copy about Democrat Margaret Louise Sanger from liveaction.org on <u>Research, Statistics, and History on Abortion & Human Rights</u>:   **Margaret Louise Sanger** (1879 – 1966) was a birth control, population control, and eugenics activist. She changed the world, but for the worse.

By 1911, Sanger had moved to New York City, where she became heavily influenced by anarchist, socialist, and labor activists. She began joining and participating in radical groups and causes.

In March 1914, Sanger published the first issue of her own paper, *The Woman Rebel*. Along with providing information about birth control, Sanger wholeheartedly supported the use of violence to achieve political, economic, and social goals. Case in point, the Lexington Avenue bombing. On July 4th of that year, a bomb accidentally exploded in a Harlem apartment, killing three men and one woman. The three men were planning to bomb the home of industrialist John D. Rockefeller, but the bomb exploded prematurely. The plan was devised at the Ferrer Center, an educational institution, which also served as the meeting place for a movement of radicals. Sanger lectured at the institution, and was active in the movement.

After the failed terrorist attempt, Sanger wrote a commentary, calling the deaths a display of "courage, determination, conviction, a spirit of defiance." She argued the "real tragedy" was "the cowardice and the poisonous respectability" of the movement's leaders who offered apologies, rather than defiance, for the episode. Sanger urged those in the movement to "accept and exult in every act of revolt against oppression," including terrorist acts. She also published a complementary article that defended the assassination of political or industrial leaders.

The following month, August 1914, Sanger was indicted for inciting murder and assassination, and for violating obscenity laws. But instead of facing the charges, she fled the country. On the trip to England, after the ship had entered international waters, Sanger instructed her supporters to distribute 100,000 copies of her pamphlet, *Family Limitation*. In February 1916, the charges were dropped. In October 1916, Sanger opened America's first birth control clinic. Located in Brownsville, New York, the clinic permanently closed a month later, after Sanger was charged with maintaining a public nuisance. In February 1917, she was convicted and given a thirty day prison sentence. Also in February 1917, the first issue of Sanger's journal, *The Birth Control Review*, was published. She was *The Review*'s editor until 1929, and used her editorials to promote birth control and eugenics. For Sanger, these issues were inseparable.

The word *eugenics*, which means *well born*, was coined in 1883 by Sir Francis Galton, a cousin of Charles Darwin. Positive eugenics was a movement that attempted to "improve" the human population by encouraging "fit" people to reproduce. Negative eugenics, conversely, attempted to "improve" the human population by discouraging "unfit" people from reproducing. The "unfit" people included the poor, the sick, the disabled, and the "feeble-minded," the "idiots," the "morons," and the "insane." And "discouragement" from reproducing included the use of force. Sanger rejected positive eugenics, while embracing negative eugenics. She wrote, "Like the advocates of Birth Control, the eugenists, for instance, are seeking to assist the race toward the elimination of the unfit. Both are seeking a single end but they lay emphasis upon different methods." She stressed the need to merge eugenics with birth control, adding, "Eugenics without Birth Control seems to us a house builded upon the sands. It is at the mercy of the rising stream of the unfit."

And Sanger advocated birth control backed up by forced sterilization or segregation to achieve her aims, writing, "While I personally believe in the sterilization of the feeble-minded, the insane and syphilitic, I have not been able to discover that these measures are more than superficial deterrents when applied to the constantly growing stream of the unfit. They are excellent means of meeting a certain phase of the situation, but I believe in regard to these, as in regard to other eugenic means, that they do not go to the bottom of the matter." The bottom of the matter was "to create a race of thoroughbreds." So the government, Sanger concluded, needed "to apply a stern and rigid policy of sterilization and segregation to that grade of population whose progeny is already tainted, or whose inheritance is such that objectionable traits may be transmitted to offspring" and "to give certain dysgenic groups in our population their choice of segregation or sterilization."

In her 1920 book, *Woman and the New Race*, Sanger wrote that birth control "is nothing more or less than the facilitation of the process of weeding out the unfit, of preventing the birth of defectives or of those who will become defectives." She had a plan. And she was about to get an organization. In 1921, Sanger founded the American Birth Control League, which (following a 1939 merger with the Birth Control Clinical Research Bureau and then a 1942 name change) became the Planned Parenthood

Federation of America. While the organization was growing, the close association between the birth control movement and the eugenics movement had made a name change necessary. Nazi Germany had implemented racial hygiene policies, including mass sterilizations, inspired by the eugenics movement in America. So "birth control" was removed from the name to create a new public image. The agenda, though, stayed the same. And in 1948, Sanger helped form the International Committee on Planned Parenthood, which (in 1952) became the International Planned Parenthood Federation.

Through it all, the underlying theme, eliminating the unfit, never changed. In her 1922 book, *The Pivot of Civilization*, she attacked charity as counterproductive, and dangerous, for helping the poor to produce even more "human waste." (Sanger's term for the children of the poor.) She wrote, "Organized charity is itself the symptom of a malignant social disease." And, "Instead of decreasing and aiming to eliminate the stocks [of people] that are most detrimental to the future of the race and the world, it tends to render them to a menacing degree dominant."

In a 1925 book, *Birth Control: Facts and Responsibilities*, Sanger contributed an essay, writing, "Birth Control is not merely an individual problem; it is not merely a national question, it concerns the whole wide world, the ultimate destiny of the human race. In his last book, Mr. [H.G.] Wells speaks of the meaningless, aimless lives which cram this world of ours, hordes of people who are born, who live, yet who have done absolutely nothing to advance the race one iota. Their lives are hopeless repetitions. All that they have said has been said before; all that they have done has been done better before. Such human weeds clog up the path, drain up the energies and the resources of this little earth. We must clear the way for a better world; we must cultivate our garden."

Then in 1926, Sanger spoke at a Ku Klux Klan rally in Silver Lake, New Jersey. Writing about the event in her autobiography, she highlighted its success, noting that "a dozen invitations to speak to similar groups" were offered.

And in 1939, Sanger went to work "cultivating the garden." She initiated the Negro Project to weed out the unfit from the black population. In bringing birth control to the then largely poor (i.e. unfit) population of the South, with a few influential black ministers promoting the project as the solution to poverty, Sanger hoped to significantly reduce the black population. Martin Luther King, Sr., as the eldest son of nine children born into poverty in a family of sharecroppers, would have made the perfect target for "elimination." But his birth had already taken place. In her later years, Sanger still believed that there were people "who never should have been born at all." In a 1957 interview with Mike Wallace, she said, "I think the greatest sin in the world is bringing children into the world – that have disease from their parents, that have no chance in the world to be a human being practically. Delinquents, prisoners, all sorts of things just marked when they're born. That to me is the greatest sin – that people can – can commit."

Sanger's impact during her lifetime was highly negative, and included the cruelty of forced sterilization, which became a common practice. In America, over 60,000 people were sterilized against their will. And most occurred during the 1930s and 1940s when Sanger and the birth control and population control movements were pushing states hard to enact and enforce compulsory sterilization laws. Among the victims were the blind, the deaf, epileptics, the mentally retarded, the mentally ill, and people with low IQs diagnosed as "feeble-minded."

Sanger's legacy today, which is being carried on by Planned Parenthood, includes the devastating impact of "birth control" on the black community. Planned Parenthood has continued the practice of targeting the black population. Over 30% of all abortions are performed on black women and close to 40% of black pregnancies end in abortion. Planned Parenthood (a strong democrat ally) successfully created a public image of an organization working to help the poor, while hiding the reality that it targets the vulnerable. That was Sanger's plan from the start.

End of copy.

Question: Which strong supporter of the Democrat Party glamorizes single parenthood, alternate lifestyles and to follow one's own interests or inclinations regardless of others. **Answer:** Hollywood and the Entertainment Industry.

ГНФЦGНГS

The Democrat party has been in control of our inner cities for the last 60 to 100 plus years. *"Two-thirds of America's 100 largest cities are controlled by Democratic Party mayors"* stated by a CNBC.com November 11th 2016 article. Our inner cities have been in a downward spiral and getting worse. Crime is rampant. Taxes are high. Quality of life is suffocating. Yet we are so brain washed that we keep voting democrat. Even if we move out of a Democrat control area and move into a more conservative area we will still vote Democrat.

We support Democrat agendas and spend our money in support of the many allies of the Democrat party (i.e., Hollywood, Music Industry, Liberal Media, etc.) blindly knowing the damage they are doing to our communities. We support them just for the scrapes they give us off their tables because we believe they have our interest at heart. Minorities must understand that a race or a group of people united under an ideology will never accept you unless you abide by their ideology or else be lambasted and excommunicated.

These Democrat political leaders live in the top quality echelon neighborhoods; they send their children to private schools, guarded by personal guards, have connections with activist justices that will jump at their commands. These Democrats have special rights and exemptions that the rest of us don't have.

Question: How do these politicians become multi-millionaires while on a public servant salary? (A typical salary for a congress person and / or a senator is $174,000 for 2016). Are there covert strings attached to their income?

With a little research, you can see who the Democrats really are and who they are beholding too. Follow the money.

The Public School Teacher's Union supports the Democrat Party 100%. They are against school choice that will free minority children to attend a better school. They opposition results in keeping minorities tied into a failing school system because they are more concern about making more money from the federal government than to allow parents to move their child to a better school for a better education. College campuses have demonstrated violently against speakers that have been invited to their colleges for an intellectual exchange of ideas but don't subscribe to liberal ideology as "Hate Speech" and have successfully prohibit them from speaking. This is not a fair exchange of ideas nor is this freedom of speech nor is this fostering an area of ideas to express intellectual thought. Liberal Democrats are Fascist in their ideology yet they believe that they are more intellectually righteous. This is the same thought process Hitler and his followers had over other belief systems and ideologies: They are right and you are wrong and you have no right to speak! Presently, hatred for law enforcement is preached and allowed on Liberal College Campuses throughout America and because of this fostering of hate by liberals about law enforcement crime is rising in minority cities because police are afraid of the rhetoric speeches in these campuses which threaten police security. Once again, minorities suffer while liberal Democrat leaders and politicians continue to live in secure neighborhoods with police protection and private security guards. Once again, Liberal Democrat politicians use minorities as puppets to further their own agendas and cement their political powers.

In 2016, the Consumer Financial Protection Bureau donated 100% of their money in support of the Democrat Party. This is the same party that gave us Dodd-Frank regulations that was crushing our community banks and local credit unions. These are the banks poor minorities go to for its free checking accounts and other services that big banks charge for. Yet, the Consumer Financial Protection Bureau will knowingly support the Democrats even though it hurts minorities.

Why did the IRS, under the misguided influence of the democrats, go after religious and conservative groups? (The IRS scandal of 2013 and 2016). Minorities, by nature, are conservative and religious. We are not liberal. But we are easily influenced by the liberal media, Hollywood and the labels that

Democrats paint their opposition with. We take it for granted that they are on our side never concluding that perhaps they are using us for the vote and manipulating us to their advantage with the help of their allies.

CIVIL RIGHTS:

Question: Why did the Democrats make themselves exempt from the Civil Rights Act of 1964? *(It was not until 1995 when the Republicans gained control of the House and Senate for the first time in forty years that the first act they passed was making Congress subject to the Civil Rights Act of 1964). While on the subject of exempt, why did the Democrats make themselves exempt from Obama-Care while toting how great it is for the rest of America?*

In regards to the Civil Rights Act of 1964, did you know that only **61%** of house Democrats and **69%** of Senate Democrats supported this legislation whereas **80%** of the house Republicans and **82%** of Senate Republicans supported the Civil Rights Act of 1964?

During the Civil Right unrest of the 1960's, southern state legislatures were under Democrat party control. They controlled most local and state officeholders in the South. These southern Democrats disenfranchised African Americans in every state of the former Confederacy at the turn of the century. Democrats had passed and maintained a series of discriminatory requirements and practices disenfranchising the millions of African Americans across the South throughout the 20th century. This led to the Civil Rights Marches of 1965 leading up to Bloody Sunday on March 7, 1965. It was Democrat Gov. George Wallace who ordered the police and police dogs to attack the marchers and it was Democrat George Wallace again that stood at the doorway of the University of Alabama to preventing African American children to integrate. The Mayor of Selma, a Democrat named Joseph Smitherman, called Martin Luther King Jr. "martin luther coon" in a televised interview in 1965. By the way, Martin Luther King Jr. was a Republican!

Some names and events you should remember that are Historical Facts:

J. William Fulbright, an Arkansas Democrat senator was eulogized by President William J. Clinton in 1995 but yet Mr. Fulbright was one of 99 Democrats who signed the Southern Manifesto of 1956 that supported segregation forever. He also filibuster the Civil Rights Act of 1964 for 83 days.

Democrat Senator Al Gore Sr. voted against the Civil Rights Act.

Democrat Senator and President Robert Byrd was a former Ku Klux Klan Exalted Cyclops.

The first seven African Americans elected to the Congress during the Reconstruction period of 1865 to 1877 were all Republicans: Senator Hiram Rhodes Revels; Representative Benjamin Turner; Representative Robert DeLarge; Representative Josiah Walls; Representative Jefferson Long; Representative Joseph Hayne Rainey and Representative Robert Brown Elliot. ***Democrats didn't elect their first African American to Congress until 1935!***

The Republican Party came together in the late 1850's as an opposition to the pro-slavery Democrat Party. The 13th amendment that abolished slavery was voted in favor for by all of the 118 Republicans in Congress while only 19 of the 82 Democrats voted for it.

For the 14th amendment that guaranteed citizenship to African Americans and for the 15th amendment granting voting rights to African Americans, **not one** Democrat voted in favor for these amendments in either the House or the Senate!

A political cartoon drawing in Harper's weekly October 21, 1876 shows two white Democrats standing alongside an African American man while pointing guns at his head. At the bottom of the drawing it read, *"Of course he wants to vote the Democratic ticket."*

Question: Why don't the Democrats march against pornography that encourages an animalistic behavior towards women? Why don't the Democrats march against the music industry that degrades women with lyrics and rhythm? (Perhaps because they support the Democrats? Research the answer).

Why don't the Democrats take an offense against criminals instead of protecting their rights over law abiding citizens? The good citizens in a minority neighborhood must spend money they don't have on greater home insurance and security measures. Why do they continue to attack the 2nd amendment? Do you know that a 2005 Supreme Court ruling ruled that law enforcement (i.e. police) has no constitutional duty to protect you?

Question: If you go to the Democrat Party website, they start their history on 1920. Why would they start their history on 1920 when their party platform goes back to 1840?

In their website, they correlate their party's history starting on 1920 with the passage of the 19th amendment, the women's right to vote. But if you dig deeper, you will find that it's another attempt to create the illusion that they were on the right side of history but the opposite is true. In 1878, California Republican Aaron A. Sargent introduced the 19th amendment permitting women to vote but was defeated by the Democrat controlled congress. Republicans continued to introduce the 19th amendment in congress every year after that which was continuously defeated by the Democrats by bottling the amendment in various committees or defeating outright on the Senate floor in 1887 with a 34 to 16 vote. Again in 1914 it was defeated by Senate Democrats and again in 1918 by a vote of 204 to 174.

In 1918 midterm elections, the Republicans sweep into power in both the House and Senate. This allowed the amendment to be passed on June 4th, 1919 and ratified on Aug 19, 1920 against the wishes of Democrat President Woodward Wilson.

Interesting to remember that the 19th amendment was passed in the House on May 21, 1919 with a 304 to 89 vote, 91% of Republicans voted for the amendment while only 59% of the Democrats voted for it.

When the amendment was passed on June 4th, 1919 in the Senate by a vote of 56 to 25, 82% of the Republicans vote for the amendment while only 41% of the Democrats voted for it. Below is a clip from the Spectator dated April 30th, 2012 on the history of the 19th Amendment:

But the Democrats' resistance was by no means dead. They did their level best to prevent the amendment from being ratified: "When the Amendment was submitted to the states, 26 of the 36 states that ratified it had Republican legislatures. Of the nine states that voted against ratification, eight were Democratic." Many of these Democrat-controlled states refused to ratify the amendment until the 1970s.

HISPANICS IN THE REPUBLICAN PARTY

1877. First Hispanic to Congress, Romualdo Pacheco. He was from California. Mexican Descent. Democrat did not have a Hispanic until 1931 and he was appointed to fill the seat vacated by the incumbent after her was killed in a plane crash.

1928. First Hispanic Senator Octaviano Larrazolo. He was from New Mexico; Mexican.

1980. First Hispanic to run for President, Ben Fernandez. He was from Kansas City, Kansas Mexican Descent.

1989. First Hispanic woman to Congress, Ileana Ros-Lehtinen. She was from Florida. Cuban-American.

1990. First Hispanic and first woman Surgeon General, Antonia Coello Novello. Born in Puerto Rico. Puerto Rican.

1995. First Hispanic Woman Governor, Susana Martinez. She was from New Mexico. Mexican Descent.

2005. First Hispanic Attorney General, Alberto Gonzales. He was from Texas. Mexican Descent.

The Democrats are continuously rewriting history with the help on the liberal media, liberal college professors, liberal talk show host and liberal Hollywood. Together, they continue to spin a web of deceit to create the illusion that they are your best advocates for your minority rights. While you fall sway to their illusion, the rest of their allies continues to take a toll on our family life. They continue to encourage a deviant lifestyle which slowly destroys the family fabric morally and financially. Hollywood loves to say that their movies are "Art imitating Life" but in actuality their movies results in "Life imitating Art" while profiting from our ignorance. The Democrats will remain silent on these issues because their biggest donor and supporter is Hollywood. In addition, this "group hug" of the good and bad elements in our neighborhoods by the Democrats creates the segmentation that minority leaders will eventually go to the Democrats for help on these community issues. The Democrats will then address these issues in terms of color, financial status, educational status, ethnicity, race, etc. etc. **This is "Self- Imposed Segmental Racism" in action.** They create the circumstances and we come to them for the solution.

FROM THE ILLUSION

THE ORIGINAL DEMOCRAT PARTY PLATFORM OF
1844 and 1848 on the question of Slavery:

7. That Congress has no power, under the Constitution, to interfere with or control the domestic institutions of the several States; and that such States are the sole and proper judges of everything pertaining to their own affairs, not prohibited by the Constitution; that all efforts, by abolitionists or others, made to induce Congress to interfere with questions of slavery, or to take incipient steps in relation thereto, are calculated to lead to the most alarming and **dangerous** consequences, and that all such efforts have an inevitable tendency to diminish the happiness of the people and endanger the stability and permanency of the Union, and ought not to be countenanced by any friend to our Political Institutions.

THE ORIGINAL DEMOCRAT PARTY PLATFORM OF 1856 on the question of Slavery:

Resolved, That we reiterate with renewed energy of purpose the well considered declarations of former Conventions upon the sectional issue of Domestic slavery, and concerning the reserved rights of the States.

1. That Congress has no power under the Constitution, to interfere with or control the domestic institutions of the several States, and that such States are the sole and proper judges of everything appertaining to their own affairs, not prohibited by the Constitution; that all efforts of the abolitionists, or others, made to induce Congress to interfere with questions of slavery, or to take incipient steps in relation thereto, are calculated to lead to the most alarming and dangerous consequences; and that all such efforts have an inevitable tendency to diminish the happiness of the people and endanger the stability and permanency of the Union, and ought not to be countenanced by any friend of our political institutions.

2. That the foregoing proposition covers, and was intended to embrace the whole subject of slavery agitation in Congress; and therefore, the Democratic party of the Union, standing on this national platform, will abide by and adhere to a faithful execution of the acts known as the compromise measures, settled by the Congress of 1850; "the act for reclaiming fugitives from service or labor," included; which act

being designed to carry out an express provision of the Constitution, cannot, with fidelity thereto, be repealed, or so changed as to destroy or impair its efficiency.

3. That the Democratic Party will resist all attempts at renewing, in Congress or out of it, the agitation of the slavery question under whatever shape or color the attempt may be made.

4. That the Democratic party will faithfully abide by and uphold, the principles laid down in the Kentucky and Virginia resolutions of 1798, and in the report of Mr. Madison to the Virginia Legislature in 1799; that it adopts those principles as constituting one of the main foundations of its political creed, and is resolved to carry them out in their obvious meaning and import.

And that we may more distinctly meet the issue on which a sectional party, subsisting exclusively on slavery agitation, now relies to test the fidelity of the people, North and South, to the Constitution and the Union—

1. Resolved, That claiming fellowship with, and desiring the co-operation of all who regard the preservation of the Union under the Constitution as the paramount issue—and repudiating all sectional parties and platforms concerning domestic slavery, which seek to embroil the States and incite to treason and armed resistance to law in the Territories; and

whose avowed purposes, if consummated, must end in civil war and disunion, the American Democracy recognize and adopt the principles contained in the organic laws establishing the Territories of Kansas and Nebraska as embodying the only sound and safe solution of the "slavery question" upon which the great national idea of the people of this whole country can repose in its determined conservatism of the Union— NON-INTERFERENCE BY CONGRESS WITH SLAVERY IN STATE AND TERRITORY, OR IN THE DISTRICT OF COLUMBIA.

As you can read, the Democrats supported and enforced the institutionalization of slavery. It was not until Republican President Abraham Lincoln issued his preliminary emancipation proclamation on September 22, 1862 that as of January 1st, 1863 all slaves shall forever be free.

THE EARLIEST ORIGINAL REPUBLICAN PARTY PLATFORM OF 1932 on the question of Slavery:

The Negro

For seventy years the Republican Party has been the friend of the American Negro. Vindication of the rights of the Negro citizen to enjoy the full benefits of life, liberty and the pursuit of happiness is traditional in the Republican Party, and our party stands pledged to maintain equal opportunity and rights for Negro citizens. We do not propose to depart from that tradition nor to alter the spirit or letter of that pledge.

REPUBLICAN PARTY PLATFORM OF 1856 on the question or Slavery:
June 18, 1856

This Convention of Delegates, assembled in pursuance of a call addressed to the people of the United States, without regard to past political differences or divisions, who are opposed to the repeal of the Missouri Compromise; to the policy of the present Administration; to the extension of Slavery into Free Territory; in favor of the admission of Kansas as a Free State; of restoring the action of the Federal Government to the principles of Washington and Jefferson; and for the purpose of presenting candidates for the offices of President and Vice-President, do

Resolved: That the maintenance of the principles promulgated in the Declaration of Independence, and embodied in the Federal Constitution are essential to the preservation of our Republican institutions, and that the Federal Constitution, the rights of the States, and the union of the States, must and shall be preserved.

Resolved: That, with our Republican fathers, we hold it to be a self-evident truth, that all men are endowed with the inalienable right to life, liberty, and the pursuit of happiness, and that the primary object and ulterior design of our Federal Government were to secure these rights to all persons under its exclusive jurisdiction; that, as our Republican fathers, when they had abolished Slavery in all our National Territory, ordained that no person shall be deprived of life, liberty, or property, without due process of law, it becomes our duty to maintain this provision **of the Constitution against all attempts to violate it for the purpose of establishing Slavery in the** Territories of the United States by positive legislation, prohibiting its existence or extension therein. That we deny the authority of Congress, of a Territorial Legislation, of any individual, or association of individuals, to give legal existence to Slavery in any Territory of the United States, while the present Constitution shall be maintained.

Resolved: That the Constitution confers upon Congress sovereign powers over the Territories of the United States for their government; and that in the exercise of this power, it is both the right and the imperative duty of Congress to prohibit in the Territories those twin relics of barbarism--Polygamy, and Slavery.

So as you can read my dear reader, the Democrats from their conception are a party of slavery, black codes, Jim Crow and the Ku Klux Klan. Even up until this day as I write this book, the Democrats are a party of terrorizing those that do not agree with them. They will label you (per Saul Alinsky rules for radicals), malign you, and call you racist and sexist and xenophobic and whatever name they can silence you with in partnership with the liberal media and Hollywood. They have been surreptitiously rewriting history and trying to keep minorities blinded to who is the real racist. It is the Democrats. They have gone underground in their methods to create an illusion that they are your friends. Meanwhile, minorities keep getting poorer, the quality of life has been getting lower, crime is worse, and education has suffered while music and movies has become predominant in our communities. Emotions and self placation of desires is the ruling guidance among minorities. Hosea 4:6. *"My people are destroyed by lack of knowledge."*

HДS

ИФГHIИG

HOW TO FIGHT THE DEMOCRATS AND FREE YOURSELF FROM THE ILLUSION.

Hillary Clinton once said that it takes a village to raise a child. The question remains: "Raise the child into what?"

I once heard a female liberal pro-democrat morning talk show host with the initials "J.B." say the Republicans has a history of racism.

I once heard a famous conservative radio talk icon say on two separate occasions that they (media, protesters, etc.) 'get their marching orders from the DNC' (Democrat National Committee) and yet on another occasion, he says that they (democrat protesters and supporters, etc.) don't need to be told what to do because of the ideology that binds them.

On March 4th, 2017 there was a national organized rally across the nation in support of President Donald Trump. In many of the rallies and one at the Ohio Statehouse in Columbus, it turned into a clash of words between pro and anti trump supporters with the anti trump supporters shouting, "No Trump, No KKK, No Fascist USA."

The above are examples of the successful surreptitious manipulations by the Democrats in the mind of their followers. They really believe that Republicans are Racist, KKK, Fascist, etc. etc. Yet, it's not the history of the Republicans but in the History of the Democrats that these labels are appropriate to.

As minority children growing up, our first initiation into politics is that Republicans are for the rich and the Democrats are for the poor. We are taught that Republicans are racist and Democrats are not. We are taught that the Democrats are common folks fighting for your rights. This indoctrination is drilled into us by our parents who also believes this too.

One of the rules from Saul Alinsky's book "Rules for Radicals," is **Rule Number 13:** *"Pick the target, freeze it, personalize it, and polarize it."*

The Democrats, along with their allies, have successfully painted the Republicans negatively with labels of racism, xenophobe, homophobe, bigot, only for the rich and against the poor, etc.

If your opposition is successful in painting you with the above negative labels, then anything you do will be met with suspicion and the trust from the people will be placed on the opposing party that is charging you with these labels. This dovetail into **Rule Number 11:** *"If you push a negative hard enough, it will push through and become a positive."* Violence from the other side can win the public to your side because the public sympathizes with the underdog.

If your party is the one that has been painted with these negative labels, you start from a negative position whereas your opponent will start from a positive position. The party with the negative image will have to contend with this unfair reputation before your listener will listen to your message. Even if you get their attention, they will listen with a skeptical and suspicious mind. While you are busy trying to shake off these negative labels, rule number 8 is played: **Rule Number 8:** *"Keep the pressure on. Never let up" keep trying new things to keep the opposition off balance. As the opposition masters one approach, hit them from the flank with something new."* The constant attacks upon the Republicans will continue from the Democrats and their allies (Hollywood, Media, etc.) to cement these negative labels in the minds of minorities and the people.

This is what has happened to the Republican Party. By taking the high moral road, these negative labels have taken hold and have become concrete in the minds of minorities and the elites. This is why the radio conservative talk show host said above is right on both counts. There are marching orders given by the DNC to certain media outlets but then there are others who don't need to hear from the DNC because they firmly believe they are fighting the good fight against the evil racist, xenophobe, bigot, fascist, KKK Republican Party who only protects the rich and not the poor.

It is our good human nature to fight against something evil. It's good (Dems) vs. evil (Reps). No one needs to give them marching orders. **Rule Number 6:** *"A good tactic is one your people enjoy."* *They'll keep doing it without urging and come back to do* *more. They're doing their thing, and will even suggest better ones.* If the people believe they are fighting against racist evil persons, they don't need marching orders.

The Democrats and their allies know that they have been successful in painting the Republicans with these negative labels. The very first interview by the newly elected DNC chairman, Tom Perez, was to call President Trump and all of his policies, **"RACIST!"** **Racism, Racism, Racism!!!**

There are some Republicans (mostly all of them in fact!) that are so afraid of these labels that they actually avoid being true to themselves and their principals just to keep from being called these negative accusations thus playing into the hands of the accusers.

The counter defense by the Republicans has been to take the high moral road and not confront these accusations and to ignore it; **"don't feed into it"** the Republicans say. They believe that they should just move forward without confronting it.

This belief of ignoring these negative labels by the democrats about them is **WRONG!** It has not help the republicans nor has it resolve itself no matter what sycophant positions Republicans take to satisfy the left leaning Democrats.

"Sometimes you got to get into it to get out of it! Sometimes you need to shake a stick at barking dogs."

Below are a few of biblical quotes that support the Republicans' need to counter these false negatives: (**Personal note:** whenever scriptures are quoted to liberal Democrats, they cringe like a vampire would cringe from a cross or from a string of garlic. Their moral compass is based on who can grant them power. I firmly believe that liberal Democrats are always looking to another person to be their savor, their king, their idol. Liberalism is their religion. Former Executive Director of the Congressional Black Caucus, Angela Rye said on CNN Anderson Cooper 360 on March 27th, 2017 that the media should be talking more about how "Barack Obama had to be the next best thing to Jesus.")

Deuteronomy 19:18-19 "The judges shall inquire diligently, and if the witness is a false witness and has accused his brother falsely, then you shall do to him as he had meant to do to his brother. So you shall purge the evil from your midst.

Matthew 18:15-17 "If your brother sins against you, go and tell him his fault, between you and him alone. If he listens to you, you have gained your brother. But if he does not listen, take one or two others along with you, that every charge may be established by the evidence of two or three witnesses. If he refuses to listen to them, tell it to the church. And if he refuses to listen even to the church, let him be to you as a Gentile and a tax collector."

Isaiah 54:17. "No weapon that is fashioned against you shall succeed, and you shall confute every tongue that rises against you in judgment. This is the heritage of the servants of the LORD and their vindication from me, declares the LORD."

These above biblical quotes have one thing in common which is the need to confront and refute false accusations!

The only way the Republicans are going to win the day against the Democrats and their allies and win the hearts of minorities is to take on this negative image and destroy it completely.

And the only way to destroy it completely is to charge the Democrats with the same negative charges that they charge the Republicans with. **We need to start fighting fire with fire! We need to muddy the waters!**

Bruce Lee, the famous martial artist, once was asked who the toughest opponent is. His answer was that the toughest opponent is the opponent who does not know anything, no technique and who comes at you kicking, scratching, biting, swinging, etc.

Republicans need to fight the Democrats as they fight you. The Republicans fight using the Queensberry rules of boxing while the Democrats attacks with kicks, scratches, bites, swings and throws the kitchen sink at us. Here is **Rule Number 5, 9 and 10** from Saul Alinskys' Rules for Radicals:

5. **"Ridicule is man's most potent weapon."** There is no defense. It's irrational. It's infuriating. It also works as a key pressure point to force the enemy into concessions.

Ridiculing also aids in subliminal messaging. **George Carlin said:**

"But when you're in front of an audience and you make them laugh at a new idea, you're guiding the whole being for the moment. No one is ever more him/herself than when they really laugh. Their defenses are down. It's very Zen-like, that moment. They are completely open, completely themselves when that message hits the brain and the laugh begins. That's when new ideas can be implanted. If a

new idea slips in at that moment, it has a chance to grow."

9. **"The threat is usually more terrifying than the thing itself."** Imagination and ego can dream up many more consequences than any activist.

   The violent rhetoric and behavior of the left as in Berkley and from Liberal Democrat politicians should not frighten the opposition to be silent nor incite minorities to behavior as the Democrats wish them to behavior. We are not puppets.

10. **"The major premise for tactics is the development of operations that will maintain a constant pressure upon the opposition."** It is this unceasing pressure that results in the reactions from the opposition that are essential for the success of the campaign.

As you can read above, the Democrats have been fighting an unconventional fight using the rules promulgated by Saul Alinsky. The Democrats have won the social media war on the Republicans because of the above tactics.

So again I repeat that the only way to destroy the Democrats' false narrative and the illusion of racism and the negative labels that is coloring the message from the Republicans is to charge the Democrats with the same negative labels that they charge the Republicans with. We need to start fighting like our opponents and learn from them.

When we charge them with the same negative accusations that they charge Republicans with, you level the playing field. This forces the media and the people to question the Republicans about the charges level at Democrats. Remember, the Democrats have a patent on the labels of racism, xenophobia, homophobia, etc. against Republicans so they won't be questioned. The Republicans will be questioned and when they are questioned about these same charges thrown at the Democrats, this serendipitous occasion will open up an opportunity for the Republicans to explain themselves. It is then that the Republicans can start breaking up this illusion by the Democrats and will win the war against the Democrats' deceit. I have used this technique many times against liberals and it always puts them on their heels because they are not used to being charged with these negative labels that they use on Republicans. Remember how Iranian leader Ruhollah Khomeini in his speech on November 5, 1979 when he described the United States as "The Great Satan"? America has always considered itself (and still is) a light of the world yet when Khomeini painted us with the Great Satan label, it put the Christian world on its heels. I remember Christian pastors alluding how our immorality is against Christ teachings. It took them aback.

During the campaign of 2016, then candidate Donald Trump made a statement that jarred the minds of both liberal Democrats and minorities. While campaigning for African-American votes, he made a simple statement. He said, *"What do you have to lose if you vote for me?"*

This simple statement psychologically punched deep into the minds of minorities and Democrats. It made minorities question his statement thus their circumstances and it also made the Democrats explain that minorities were happy under their influence. The Illusion took a blow.

We need to put the Democrats on defense by mudding up the waters and charging them with what they charge us with. Only this way can we begin to destroy their illusion that has covered the minds of the uninformed. If, as a Republican, you cannot defend your revertible charges back onto the democrats, then you need to get out of your bubble and come back down to street level and learn the truth of their deceptive ways.

Below are some talking points on particular issues that might help stimulate your creativity to counter the negative labels that the Democrats have successfully painted the Republican with:

On Racism: The history of the Democrats' Party is a history of anti-civil rights, anti-women's rights, KKK, Jim Crow Laws, black codes and slavery. The modern day Democrats spins the illusion that they are advocates for minority rights but in reality their policies inflicts a subculture of ignorance and immorality. They accomplish this by protecting rights of criminals, higher taxes and interest rates that is a form of financial slavery. They immune themselves from policies that they want the rest of Americans to follow such as in Obama-care and previously the Civil Rights Act. They trap minorities into failing schools by opposing School Vouchers only to placate the Teacher's Union over the future of minority children. The Democrats will not oppose their allies in Hollywood which continues to glorify violence and abhorrent behaviors in minority neighborhoods because Hollywood is a big contributor to the Democrat Party. As a minority, if you dare go against them they will label you racial derogatory terms such as "Coconut" and "Uncle Tom" and "Traitor." They can easily fight against the degrading nature of pornography and the easy accessibility of adult films on the internet by restricting the access of these movies and videos with common sense laws (i.e. adult websites must be .XXX) but the adult industry is a big contributor to the Democrat Party. Here is what Porno mogul Larry Flynt told The Wrap on Aug. 19th, 2015: "I'm endorsing Hillary Clinton," Hustler magazine publisher Larry Flynt tells The Wrap. "If she wins, she'll be able to appoint two or three judges to the Supreme Court, which could shift the balance." The appointment of judges could be critical for pornographers in the 2016 election cycle, particularly when it comes to privacy issues, piracy, and net neutrality.

The harmful effects of the music industry, which is also a big democrat contributor, and the porn industry have destroyed the minds of minorities by subjecting them to forces of animalistic appetites and consumerism.

On Homophobia: The Democrats are masters in hiding their agenda. People in general want to be left alone to worship as they please, to have sex with whoever they please as long as its adults. Yet, the Democrats takes a specific group, makes them a victim, raise them up to a higher level than the ordinary citizen of this country, force upon the rest of us the lifestyle of this victimized group in all portions of our lives then continues to push and push knowing full well that this action will result in animosity and push back. Live and let live. Would the gay movement like it if the government forces them to hear religious sermons in all of their gatherings? The protection of our rights is in our constitution but the Democrats will push to legislate a behavior upon others that wants just to be left alone. If you reject it because of your own private beliefs, the liberal Democrats will right away paint you with Homophobia and Racist. They love to divide and conquer.

On Xenophobia: The definition of Xenophobia is an intense or irrational dislike or fear of people from other countries. The history of the Democrats is the love of other people so much that they love to put them in chains or servitude like they have done to the African-American whether its physical chains or economic servitude due to high taxes, less jobs, low wages.

Democrats present an image of tolerance but in actuality, they are intolerant of people and cultures. They and their allies love presenting minorities or other cultures in a light that they have painted for them via Hollywood movies and the media. They don't care who comes into the country as long as it will favor them in the ballot box to keep them in power. They open the country to Mexican illegal immigrants because they know they can manipulate them to vote Democrat but they have eliminated the "Wet foot, Dry foot" policy of Cubans because they know in general Cubans vote Republicans. Coming from a communist country, Cubans know that the

Democrats and the communist ideology are one side of the same coin.

On Labor: Socialism is a Democrats' paradise. "Workers of the world unite" is a communist motto that suggests that the people who have wealth are enemies of the have-nots. Wealth to the Democrats is anyone who has more than they define. In the eyes of the Democrats, those that produce and own businesses are enemies of the working class. They see economics as a finite pie: "the bigger your slice is, the less for the rest of us." They don't see economics as a dynamic, growing, changing system with infinite possibilities and expansion. Socialism, where ever it's been tried, fails because it creates a two-class system and not the three-class system we have in our country. The two-classes are the rich and the poor. The rich makes the rules and the poor follows them. The Democrats ideology is all about government in charge. They become rich while telling you how to live your life with the scrapes they allow you to have. But if you support them, they will let you grow. Go against them, and they will make sure to break you (i.e., use of the IRS, Labor Regulations, etc.).

Wikipedia Fact: The **Norris–La Guardia Act** (also known as the **Anti-Injunction Bill**) is a 1932 United States federal law on US labor law.[1] It banned yellow-dog contracts, barred the federal courts from issuing injunctions against nonviolent labor disputes, and created a positive right of noninterference by employers against workers joining trade unions. The common title comes from the names of the sponsors of the legislation: Senator George W. Norris of Nebraska and Representative Fiorello H. La Guardia of New York, both Republicans. The Act states that yellow-dog contracts, where workers agree as a condition of employment to not join a labor union, are unenforceable in federal court. It also establishes that employees are free to form unions without employer interference and prevents the federal courts from issuing injunctions in nonviolent labor disputes. The three provisions include protecting worker's self-organization and liberty or "collective bargaining", removing jurisdiction from federal courts vis-a-vis the issuance of injunctions in non-violent labor disputes, and outlawing the "yellow-dog" contract.

From Punkerslut.com: The 1932 Norris-LaGuardia Act passed by the Republican-dominated legislature protected workers; the 1935 NLRB Act passed by a Democrat-dominated legislature protected capitalists. Both of them are worded the same and offer the same guarantees to the workers. But the NLRB creates an essentially new and autocratic branch of the government that is certainly not representative of the people in any legal sense, yet it rules over them. The Labor Relations Board is a theoretical defense of the workers, but like the state-run unions of the Soviet Union and China, its practice is actually the oppression of the workers.

One other difference should be noted between the Norris-LaGuardia Act and the NLRB. The Norris-LaGuardia Act applies to all workers, everywhere, under any jurisdiction, for whatever purposes. The NLRB divided and sub-divided the working-class into different components, excluding some and accepting others. The agricultural workers were excluded, for instance. The primary supporter of the bill among labor was the American Federation of Labor, and since this union refuses to deal with "industrial workers" and "unskilled manual labor," there was no need to cover agricultural workers. Servants were also excluded. Other groups were excluded, as well...

"...[this law] shall not include any individual employed as an agricultural laborer, or in the domestic service of any family or person at his home, or any individual employed by his parent or spouse, or any individual having the status of an independent contractor, or any individual employed as a supervisor, or any individual employed by an employer subject to the Railway Labor Act [45 U.S.C. 151 et seq.], as amended from time to time, or by any other person who is not an employer as herein defined."

Democrats love to divide and conquer by breaking society in segments then pitting one against the other. At one time, when you saw a successful person, you would tell your child, "If you study and work hard, you can be just as successful." But nowadays, when we see a successful person, we call him or her evil, selfish, and we demand from their wealth. We become jealous. The Democrats and their allies have created this mindset but yet you see that they themselves become rich and wealthy while pointing their fingers to others as the reason you are not. This is a form of racism because it is prejudice against the natural inclination in a person to earn from his or her initiative and to develop their character. Don't be fooled by the illusion the Democrats spin about being friends with labor. They are the party of Globalism and they will always allow our jobs to be shipped overseas or allow foreign corporations to bleed our labor force. During the presidential campaign of 2016, Democrat Candidate Hillary Clinton was endorsed by John Bachtell who is the head of the Communist Party USA. The Communist Party ideology is the party that produced Stalin and Mao. These advocates of the Communist philosophy are responsible for the death of 85 to 100 million people because they did not toe the party line and accept communism as an ideology or lifestyle. The Democrat Party and the Communist Party are one side of the same coin. Just look at the violence and the "brown-shirt" tactics from the Democrats and their allies towards anyone who voted for Trump for the Presidency. They have used physical, financial, political, judicial, threats and career ending tactics if you voted for or supported anyone other than Hillary Clinton. Presently, these tactics have all been recorded and is part of our history for the 2016 Presidential Campaign. This, of course, will eventually become extinct and ignored by the media, Hollywood and liberal College Professors in years to come.

Proverbs chapter 10:4 & 22. *"The lazy person becomes poor. The busy person becomes rich."*

"God gives wealth to the man who pleases him. And that man's wealth will not cause him any trouble.

It was the Democrats and the liberal allies in the Teachers' Union that took God and the commandments from out of the public classrooms and replaced it with their liberal ideology for the collective good. The majority of atheist and anarchist are Democrats and / or support the Democrats.

<u>On Fascism:</u> Former President Ronald Reagan, in a 1975 interview with CBS correspondent Mike Wallace, said, *"You know, someone very profoundly once said many years ago that if fascism ever comes to America, it will come in the name of liberalism. And what is fascism? Reagan said. "Fascism is private ownership, private enterprise, but total government control and regulation. Well, isn't this the liberal philosophy? The conservative, so-called, is the one that says less government, get off my back, get out of my pocket, and let me have more control of my own*

destiny," he said. Liberalism is a fascist ideology. The paragraphs below are what the Democrats love to do when they are in power:

From the library of economics and liberty:
As an economic system, fascism is **socialism** with a capitalist veneer. The word derives from *fasces,* the Roman symbol of collectivism and power: a tied bundle of rods with a protruding ax. In its day (the 1920s and 1930s),

Under fascism, the state, through official **cartels**, controlled all aspects of manufacturing, commerce, finance, and agriculture. Planning boards set product lines, production levels, prices, wages, working conditions, and the size of firms. Licensing was ubiquitous; no economic activity could be undertaken without government permission. Levels of consumption were dictated by the state, and "excess" incomes had to be surrendered as taxes or "loans." The consequent burdening of manufacturers gave advantages to foreign firms wishing to export. But since government policy aimed at autarky, or national self-sufficiency, **protectionism** was necessary: imports were barred or strictly controlled, leaving foreign conquest as the only avenue for access to resources unavailable domestically. Fascism was thus incompatible with peace and the international division of labor—hallmarks of liberalism.

From livescience.com:

Fascism is a complex ideology. There are many definitions of fascism; some people describe it as a type or set of political actions, a political philosophy or a mass movement. Paxton, author of several books, including "The Anatomy of Fascism" (Vintage, 2005), said fascism is based more on feelings than philosophical ideas. In his 1988 essay "The Five Stages of Fascism," published in 1998 in the Journal of Modern History, he defined seven feelings that act as "mobilizing passions" for fascist regimes. They are:

1. The primacy of the group. Supporting the group feels more important than maintaining either individual or universal rights.

2. Believing that one's group is a victim. This justifies any behavior against the group's enemies.

3. The belief that individualism and liberalism enable dangerous decadence and have a negative effect on the group.

4. A strong sense of community or brotherhood. This brotherhood's "unity and purity are forged by common conviction, if possible, or by exclusionary violence if necessary."

5. Individual self-esteem is tied up in the grandeur of the group. Paxton called this an "enhanced sense of identity and belonging."

6. Extreme support of a "natural" leader, who is always male. This results in one man taking on the role of national savior.

7. "The beauty of violence and of will, when they are devoted to the group's success in a Darwinian struggle," Paxton wrote. The idea of a naturally superior group or, especially in Hitler's case, biological racism, fits into a fascist interpretation of Darwinism.

THE BOTTOM LINE.

All parties should learn from the Democrats. Democrats never throw their own under the bus nor do they fight or expose each other publicly. They stand united because they believe that they are right and the rest of us are wrong or not enlightened. They never blame themselves for failures but always blame others for not understanding their policies or thinking. Parties, other than the Democrats, must learn to really believe in their own belief system and also be willing to settle and accept partial enactment of their policies because the Democrats did not arrive at this point in time by throwing everything out there all at once. It was a slow process but a constant striving, with the help of their allies, to achieve their goals. Rome was not built in a day. The Sun does not pop-up in the morning. It is a gradual ascension. Republicans would do well to apply this natural pattern in all of their policies. Expect the Democrats and their allies to cry, scratch, scream, kick and do every dirty trick in the book to stop this progression. They love power and they feed off of power. When they act like this, with the support of their media, it is not the time to award them by giving in to their demands unless you are worried about your own power status. The reality is that Republicans give in to the Democrats not because of the Democrat party but because Republicans are afraid of the liberal media and Hollywood. Giving in to the Democrats is giving in to their powerful allies, Hollywood, media, globalist, etc.

Every time Republicans give in, they make the Democrat allies stronger and in charge of the moral compass of America.

Question: The word *"Democrat"* is used to describe a member of the Democratic Party. When the Democrats have their party convention, they call it the *"Democratic Party Convention."*

Yet, why is it that the word *"Republican"* is used to describe a member of the Republican Party and when they have their convention, they still call it the *"Republican Party Convention"* rather than the *"Republic Convention"*? The Democrats won't call their convention the *"Democrats Party Convention"*. The word *"Republicans"* has an anathema connotation to it perpetrated by decades of negative reinforcement via the media. Republicans will do well to change their convention to *"Republic."* They should not expect the Democrats to call their convention the *"Democrats Convention"* because the word *"Democrats"* can also have a negative connotation to it more so than the word *"Democratic"* which will never be negative to most people.

THE UNIFICATION OF THE RELIGIONS.

The Churches, Mosques, Temples and other religious entities must unite to fight the destructive onslaught of the Democrats' liberal policies or they will find themselves controlled by elitist and an atheistic behavior that believes religion is a problem rather than a solution to humanity. Religion has no place in a communist country because communism, by its nature, is wholly based on the intellect (albeit faulty) rather than the spiritual side of human nature. They call religion the drug of the masses. Isn't this an elitist attitude? Isn't this the same attitude of our present day liberals? Don't they believe that they are more evolved, more understanding, more loving than those who follow scriptures which they love to label as backwards with no real place in modern day society except only to placate the dying (if weak and needy). I have heard Democrats say that Jesus is with them because they help the poor. The Democrats definition of helping the poor is keeping them poor so that the Democrats can always stay in power. Why would they want you to be wealthy and independent when it would result in you not in need of them? Jesus taught self-accountability: Matt. 16:24 "take up your cross" means taking up your responsibility. Also read Matt. 25:15-30 on a parable about responsibility and accountability.

A story: 3 blind men went to a circus never been there before or know any of the animals. They were presented with an elephant. One blind man felt its trunk. The second blind man felt its side. The third blind man felt its tail. Later upon returning home, they were asked to describe an elephant. The one blind man described it as a large round tube. The second blind man describes it as a solid fleshy wall. The third blind man describes it as a thin long rod.

The moral of this story is that all religions have something good to offer and if we put that goodness together, perhaps we can all get a better picture of God and who he is and what he want from us.

Religious organizations can have a commonality that will help society thrive as opposed to the godless liberal ideology of the Democrats and their allies.

RULES FOR RADICALS BY SAUL ALINSKY.

This book was written by Saul Alinsky in 1971 and in his introductory page, he writes the following:

"Lest we forget at least an over-the-shoulder acknowledgment to the very first radical: from all our legends, mythology, and history (and who is to know where mythology leaves off and history begins — or which is which), the first radical known to man who rebelled against the establishment and did it so effectively that he at least won his own kingdom — Lucifer."

— SAUL ALINSKY.

To think that God the Creator, the Powerful, the All Knowing cannot stop or not be in control of his creation (i.e., Lucifer) is spiritual stupidity. Is it any wonder that atheist and anarchist have a proclivity to the Democrats party?

GET TO KNOW THESE RULES. THESE ARE THE RULES THAT THE DEMOCRATS AND THEIR ALLIES WILL USE AGAINST YOU!

1. "Power is not only what you have, but what the enemy thinks you have." Power is derived from 2 main sources – money and people. "Have-Nots" must build power from flesh and blood.
2. "Never go outside the expertise of your people." It results in confusion, fear and retreat. Feeling secure adds to the backbone of anyone.
3. "Whenever possible, go outside the expertise of the enemy." Look for ways to increase insecurity, anxiety and uncertainty.
4. "Make the enemy live up to its own book of rules." If the rule is that every letter gets a reply, send 30,000 letters. You can kill them

with this because no one can possibly obey all of their own rules.

5. "Ridicule is man's most potent weapon." There is no defense. It's irrational. It's infuriating. It also works as a key pressure point to force the enemy into concessions.

6. "A good tactic is one your people enjoy." They'll keep doing it without urging and come back to do more. They're doing their thing, and will even suggest better ones.

7. "A tactic that drags on too long becomes a drag." Don't become old news.

8. "Keep the pressure on. Never let up." Keep trying new things to keep the opposition off balance. As the opposition masters one approach, hit them from the flank with something new.

9. "The threat is usually more terrifying than the thing itself." Imagination and ego can dream up many more consequences than any activist.

10. "The major premise for tactics is the development of operations that will maintain a constant pressure upon the opposition." It is this unceasing pressure that results in the reactions from the opposition that are essential for the success of the campaign.

11. "If you push a negative hard enough, it will push through and become a positive." Violence from the other side can win the

public to your side because the public sympathizes with the underdog.

12. "The price of a successful attack is a constructive alternative." Never let the enemy score points because you're caught without a solution to the problem.

13. "Pick the target, freeze it, personalize it, and polarize it." Cut off the support network and isolate the target from sympathy. Go after people and not institutions; people hurt faster than institutions.

THE SYMBOL OF THE DEMOCRAT PARTY

Brief History:

The symbol can be traced back to the 1828 presidential campaign of Andrew Jackson. His opponents tagged his last name as "Jack-ass" (donkey) because of Mr. Jackson's stubbornness.

Andrew Jackson spun it to his advantage as a "strong-willed" animal with loyalty and perseverance. He plastered a drawing of a donkey on his campaign posters.

My take on the symbol of the Democrats: The Democrats like to say that Jesus said to take care of the poor. They also take pride in the donkey as the symbol of the Democrats Party since Jesus rode on one. Symbolically the donkey is stubborn, persistent, has much endurance to resist, needs taming and is ignorant of its true spiritual self. It has a very loud voice (brags).

This symbol was originally used along the African Nile Valley to show the battles and struggle between divine man and animalistic man. Jesus (a symbol of righteousness) riding the donkey represents riding in on the spiritual ignorance of the people and / or the animalistic nature of man. Jesus guided the donkey to his destination. We must be guided and mastered by the higher moral intellect of our souls.

Conclusion: In order to be free and achieve our true nature as a people, the righteous must continue to confront the Democrat's illusion that has distorted the vision of minorities. A lack of vision or a vision that is distorted will destroy a people, a race. The Democrats love enforcing the belief among

minorities that we are not part of the American dream. The Democrats are stubborn and has the loudest of all political voices but regardless of their behavior, confronting them is a must by all concerning individuals that desire freedom and intellectual growth.

As I stated in my introduction, neither party is 100% right or 100% wrong. The Republicans are not 100% right but neither are they 100% wrong. The Democrats are not 100% right but neither are they 100% wrong. But it's only the Democrats who wants minorities to think that they are 100% right and that their policies are the only right policies for minorities. We, as minorities, cannot let the Democrats think that our votes will continue to be just for them. Nor can we let them believe that we will always settle for whatever policy they want us to have. Whatever they do for us, we must ask, *"what is in it for them?"* If they say that they are doing it out of the goodness of their hearts...then why? Is it guilt? More power? Influence? Is it some type of payback or some type of financial advantage to their allies or themselves? What are the end results of their policies on us? Does it elevate us to be better human beings? Better family life? Who is actually benefiting?

These and other questions must be asked to the party that claims that they are for minorities. Remember, they are civil servants; servants of the people. The people are us.

SAYINGS AND BELIEFS TO REMEMBER

"Republicans are for both the man and the dollar, but in case of conflict the man before the dollar."
Abraham Lincoln

"We the people are the rightful masters of both Congress and the courts, not to overthrow the Constitution but to overthrow the men who pervert the Constitution." **Abraham Lincoln**

"America will never be destroyed from the outside. If we falter and lose our freedoms, it will be because we destroyed ourselves." **Abraham Lincoln**

"The shepherd drives the wolf from the sheep's for which the sheep thanks the shepherd as his liberator, while the wolf denounces him for the same act as the destroyer of liberty. Plainly, the sheep and the wolf are not agreed upon a definition of liberty." **Abraham Lincoln**

"Labor is prior to, and independent of, capital. Capital is only the fruit of labor, and could never have existed if labor had not first existed. Labor is the superior of capital, and deserves much the higher consideration." **Abraham Lincoln**

"To educate a man in mind and not in morals is to educate a menace to society." **Theodore Roosevelt**, (1858-1919) 26th US President

The Ten Cannots of William J. H. Boetcker. Mr. Boetcker was an American religious leader and influential public speaker.

There are several minor variants but the most commonly accepted version is below:

- *You cannot bring about prosperity by discouraging thrift.*
- *You cannot strengthen the weak by weakening the strong.*
- *You cannot help little men by tearing down big men.*
- *You cannot lift the wage earner by pulling down the wage payer.*
- *You cannot help the poor by destroying the rich.*
- *You cannot establish sound security on borrowed money.*
- *You cannot further the brotherhood of man by inciting class hatred.*
- *You cannot keep out of trouble by spending more than you earn.*
- *You cannot build character and courage by destroying men's initiative and independence.*
- *And you cannot help men permanently by doing for them what they can and should do for themselves.*

This book is
dedicated to
minorities across this
great land of ours
who wish to be free
from the Democrats'
plantation and the
illusion of deception.

END.